John R. Carter

Questions in Natural and Revealed Religion

John R. Carter

Questions in Natural and Revealed Religion

ISBN/EAN: 9783337828714

Printed in Europe, USA, Canada, Australia, Japan

Cover: Foto ©Lupo / pixelio.de

More available books at **www.hansebooks.com**

QUESTIONS

IN

Natural and Revealed

RELIGION:

A COMPILATION

BY

Rev. John Pym Carter, A. M.

•••

BALTIMORE·
WM. J. CARTER & CO., PRINTERS,
75 West Fayette Street.
1882.

INTRODUCTION.

RELIGION -- ITS ORIGIN AND DIVISIONS.

1. *What is Religion?*—Religion is the service and worship due from man to God his infinite and glorious Creator.

2. *What is the etymology of the word religion?*—It is derived from the Latin *Religio:* (*ligo* to bind and *re* again;) a word adopted by the Romans to express the many obligations to which they bound themselves in the oft repeated vows, oaths, sacrifices, &c. in which the service of their imaginary gods chiefly consisted.

3. *Is religion a divine institution or is it a human invention?*—Although some ignorant and infidel men have maintained that religion is a human invention devised by kings and priests to keep men in subjection to their authority, yet every candid mind must admit that it is a divine institution.

4. *How does it appear that religion is a divine instituton?*—(1.) From the fact that man is endowed with faculties which render him capable of religion and which incline him to its exercise. (2.) All nations have some form of religion. (3.) God has revealed himself as the Creator, Ruler, and Redeemer of men and has commanded us to love and serve him.

5. *How many kinds of religion are there?*—Two kinds: true religion and false religion.

6. *In what does true religion consist?*—In the worship and service of God according to his revealed will.

7. *What is false religion?*—It is the worship of creatures, real or imaginary, such as idols or false gods; or the worship of the true God in any way not divinely appointed.

8. *Which is the more ancient, true religion or false religion?*—True religion: false religion being a departure from the original true religion, or a more or less gross corruption of it. Cain's *unbloody offering*, not expressing faith in the promised Redeemer, (Heb. 9: 7, 15, 22; 11: 4, 6,) appears to have been the first deviation from the true religion. Ninus or Belus the founder of Babylon, (B. C. 2,217,) introduced the worship of the heavenly bodies, using the Tower of Babel as an astrological observatory. And Ninus his son and successor made an image of his father Belus, which he caused the people to worship.

9. *How did false religion originate?*—In rebellion against Gods's supreme authority, and in hatred of his pure and holy character. (Exod. ch. 35; I. Kings, ch. 11; II. Kings, 17: 5–33: Rom. 1: 18–25; 28–32; I. Cor. 10: 19–21; I. Tim. 4: 1–3.)

10. *What are the character and influence of false religion?*—It is earthly, sensual, and audacious; deceptive, corrupting, and ruinous.

11. *How has the true religion been made known to man?*—In the works of creation and providence; and in the Inspired Scriptures of the Old and New Testaments; giving rise to the distinction between *Natural* and *Revealed Religion*.

NATURAL RELIGION.

1. *What is Natural Religion?*—It is that religious truth which our unassisted reason may learn from the works of creation and providence.

2. *What particular doctrines are thus discernable by the light of nature?*—Two of the most important, viz : 1st, That there is but one only living and true God, who is infinite in being and perfection. 2d, That there is a moral law of God, which, all men having violated, demands our punishment.

3. *In what manner does the light of nature teach the existence of God the Creator?*—As we naturally believe that "every house is builded by some man," so we as naturally believe, that "He who built all things is God." (Heb. 3: 3, 4.) (*Appendix Note A.*)

4. *How is this point stated in the Scriptures?*—Psalm 19: 1—3; Rom. 1: 19, 20.

5. *In what part of God's works is the moral law more particularly made known?*—In the sentiments of our conscience, (Rom. 2: 14, 15;) and by our natural instincts, (Jude, verse 10.)

6. *What may we learn from the course of God's providence?*—Acts 14: 15—17; 17: 22—31.

7. *By what other passages of Scripture are these important truths confirmed and illustrated?*—Deut. 6: 4; Neh. 9: 6; Job 11: 7—9; 26: 14; 31: 26—28; Ps. 36: 6; 104: 24—33; Jer. 10: 10; I. Cor. 8: 4—6; I. Thess. 1: 9.

8. *What forms of error are opposed to the great truths of natural religion?*—1st, *Atheism,* which denies the existence of God; 2d, *Pantheism,* which denies the

distinct personality of God; 3d, *Dualism*, which is belief in two gods; 4th, *Polytheism*, which is belief in many gods.

9. *What is Atheism?*—The name *atheism* is derived from two Greek words, *a*, without, and *theos*, God; and it designates that form of infidelity which denies the existence of God.

10. *What must be the character of a person that entertains so absurd and blasphemous an opinion as atheism?*—Being without God, without religion, and without hope, his life must be one of blank and base selfishness; little, if at all, elevated above that of the beasts of the field.

11. *Has atheism ever extensively prevailed?*—So unreasonable is this repulsive form of error, and so opposed is it to the common sentiments of mankind upon this subject, that comparatively few have ventured to assert their disbelief of their Maker's existence. Indeed, it has been questioned, whether there ever was, or can be, an atheist.

12. *What considerations show that it is possible for men to be atheists?*—We are informed, (Rom. 1: 28,) that when men did not like to retain God in their knowledge, God gave them over to a reprobate mind. And in that reprobate mind, they not only "changed the glory of the uncorruptible God, into an image made like to corruptible man, and to birds and four-footed beasts, and creeping things," (Rom. 1: 23;) but are fully competent to go to the extent of folly and blasphemy, saying in their hearts, "There is no God," (Psalm 14;) or while they profess to know him, deny him in their works, being "abominable, and disobedient, and unto every good work reprobate, (Titus 1: 16.) And thus we have atheism speculative, and atheism practical, in one or both forms of which, it has undoubtedly existed; and, it is to be feared, may still be found among men.

13. *In what form was atheism held by some ancient philosophers?*—Among the ancients, atheism was held by the Epicurean philosophers, who taught, that while there were superior beings called gods, yet they could have nothing to do with the creation or government of the world; for that would require so much care and attention, it would destroy all their happiness. Their philosophy, therefore, denied the existence of God, the Creator and Governor of all things; who, while upholding all things by the word of his power, is at the same time, "The Blessed and only Potentate, the King of kings, and Lord of lords."

14. *By whom in later times has atheism been professed?* By Spinoza an infidel Jew of Amsterdam, who for his blasphemy, was condemned and banished, A. D., 1675; by Vanani, a native of Naples, who, for the same crime, was in 1619, burned at Toulouse; and by the Budhists of Southern India, China, and Japan.

15. *How did the more eminent ancient philosophers regard atheism?*—Cicero, Seneca, and other eminent heathen philosophers have triumphantly exposed the absurdity and wickedness of atheism. Their arguments are 1st, "Consensus populorum omnium probat Deum esse."—"The consent of all people proves the existence of God." And 2nd, "Agnoscimus Deum ex operibus ejus."-We acknowlege God from his works.

16. *What is Pantheism?*—The derivation of this word from *pan*, all, *theos*, god, indicates that form of error which denies the existence of the infinite and eternal Being, who is personally distinct from all other beings, and independent of all his works; and maintains, that god is nothing more than the mere general active principle of nature, giving rise to all the motions, changes, and other phenomena of the material world; and producing all the thoughts, words, and actions of men.

17. *By whom has this form of error been adopted?*
By some of the old Grecian philosophers, by the Brahmins of Hindostan, and by some infidels of the present time, who have ignorantly embraced this ancient absurdity, and maintained it, as though it were the recent discovery of their superior genius.

18. *What may be observed respecting this shocking form of error?*—That it not only denies the distinct and independent personal existence of our glorious Creator, but it also destroys all our personal character and responsibility, confounds vice with virtue ; and in effect, makes the pure and holy God the real and immediate author of all sin ; and thus is it utterly at war with the common sense and conscience of men.

19. *What is Dualism?*—It is belief in two gods : a form of error adopted by the ancient Persians, by Manes and a few other heretics. One god whom the Persians believed to be the author of all good, they named Ormusd, and the other, whom they considered the author of all evil, they named Ahriman.

20. *Wherein appears the absurdity of this error?*
1st, Since there is in nature, an evident unity of plan and oneness of design and purpose ; the existence of more than one Creator is improbable. 2d, Since the production of any part of creation must have required the exercise of infinite power, that infinite power was competent to produce the whole ; the existence of more than one Creator is therefore unnecessary. 3d, And since the Creator who is in any respect infinite, can have, in that respect, no equal ; the existence of more than One Infinite God, the Creator, is impossible.

21. *What is the teaching of the Scriptures on this subject?*—In general, that Jehovah is the sole Creator of all things, (Gen. 1 : 1–5. John 1 : 1–3.) And in particular, the Lord, by the Prophet Isaiah, addressing the king of Persia, says : "I am the Lord, and

there is none else, there is no God besides me." * * * ": form the light, and create darkness: I make peace and create evil; I the Lord do all these things."— (Isiah 45 : 1–7.)

22. *What was the system of Manes?*—Manes or Manichœus, a Persian, on becoming a Christian, undertook to explain the doctrines of the Bible on the principles of the Persian dualism. He taught among other things, that Jehovah the God of light and peace, and Satan the God of darkness and evil, are independent of each other; and are continually at war. That the souls of men, which proceeded from the God of light, were captured by the God of darkness, and by him were imprisoned in material bodies; and so were subjected to sin and misery—that Christ, (who, himself, had no real body, but only a mere shadowy appearance of a body,) was sent to rescue souls from their imprisonment in clay—that the perfection of Christian life consists in a rigorous abstinence from all bodily appetites and pleasures, in seclusion from the world, fastings, &c.—and that Manes himself, was the Comforter promised by Christ.

23. *In what form do these errors still remain?*— Although the sect of the Maniches as a distinct body, has long since disappeared, yet their fanatical and extravagant follies remain in the rigors of monastic life, the prohibition of marriage, penances, indulgences, and other unscriptural delusions.

24. *What is Polytheism?*—It is the belief in many gods.

25. *What was probably the orgin of the heathen belief in many Gods?*—The fabulous traditions representing the exploits of heroes and other eminent men and women; and the imagination of the ancient poets in describing virtues vices and the phenomena of nature as though they were living beings. These personifications of inanimate things, although

at first probably intended to be mere symbols, came in process of time to be regarded as actual living divinities; and as such, properly objects of worship. And that worship, by an easy transition, was soon transferred to the idols which were supposed to represent the imaginary deities. To the worship and service of such vanities were men abandoned because they did not like to retain in their minds the knowledge of the true God.—(Acts, 7: 39–43; Rom. 1: 21-25. Intro. Quests. 2, 8, 9.)

26. *How did the Apostle Paul expose the folly of the Athenians in worshipping idols?*—Acts, 17: 22—29. See also I. Cor. 8: 4—7.

27. *What important thought is suggested to the reflecting mind by the great truths of natural religion?*—The necessity for more light. For while the light of nature so far manifests the existence and the law of God, as to render sin inexcusable; yet it affords no intimation upon what terms sin may be pardoned; and is wholly silent upon many other subjects of the deepest interest to mankind.

28. *Where have we a full and satisfactory revelation of the truth respecting all these important matters?*—In the Scriptures of the Old and New Testaments.

REVEALED RELIGION.

THE BIBLE--ITS INSPIRATION.

1. *What is Revealed Religion?*—It is that knowledge of God and of his will which is recorded in the Bible.

2. *What is the meaning of the word Bible?*—It is from the Greek, *Biblos*, book, and it is the name given to the volume containing the word of God; and hence, the most important book in the world.

3. *By what other name is the Bible called?*—The Holy Scriptures or Writings.

4. *Why called Holy Scriptures?*—Because they were written by holy men, who were inspired by the Holy Spirit, to teach men holiness.

5. *By what texts of Scripture is this proved?*—II. Tim. 3 : 16, 17. "All Scripture is given by inspiration of God, and is profitable for doctrine, for reproof, for correction, for instruction in righteousness: that the man of God may be perfect, thoroughly furnished unto all good works." II. Peter. 1 : 21. "For the prophecy came not in old time by the will of man: but holy men of God spake as they were moved by the Holy Ghost."

6. *Who then, is really the author of the Bible?*—God, our Heavenly Father.

7. *In what sense, and to what extent, is God the author of the Bible?*—God revealed to his holy prophets and apostles, not only the things they were to record, but also, the identical words they were to use.

8. *How is this proved?*—By such texts as Exodus, 20 : 1. "And God spake all *these words*," &c., in which the sacred writers use the very words that

were uttered by the Almighty. In other cases, the Holy Spirit evidently directed them what words to use.

9. *By what other method besides the use of words, was the truth occasionally revealed to the prophets?*—By symbolic representations presented in visions or trances; and these symbols naturally suggested the words required to describe them. (Gen. 15: 17—19; Isa. 6: 1—7; Ezek. 1: 4; Dan. 7, and the Book of Revelation throughout.)

10. *How was the inspiration of the prophets at first demonstrated?*—They explicitly asserted that they were commissioned to make known the will of God; they wrought miracles or delivered prophecies in the name of the Lord; and their divine inspiration was fully recognized by competent judges: such as that of the Old Testament prophets by the Jewish nation; and that of the apostles and writers of the New Testament, by the multitudes that witnessed their miraculous gifts, and by the churches to which their writings were addressed. (*Append. Note, B.*)

11. *What is a Miracle?*—A Miracle is an exercise of supreme control over the known and usual laws of nature, by the power of God, interposed in testimony of the mission of a prophet. (Exod. 4: 2—5; John, 5: 36; 10: 25, 37, 38; Acts, 14: 3.)

12. *How do miracles prove the divine mission of a professed prophet?*—Because no man can perform miracles except God be with him. (John, 3: 2; 9: 30—33.) (*Append. Note, C.*)

13. *What is a Prophecy?*—A Prophecy is the foretelling of an event which could not have been foreseen without divine assistance.

14. *What inference necessarily follows from the fulfilment of Prophecy?*—That the prophets must have been inspired with the knowledge of the future, by

the Holy Spirit of that Divine Being who designs and orders a l things from the beginning. (Acts, 15: 18.) (*Append. Note, D.*)

15. *What evidences of Divine Inspiration, do we find in the Scriptures themselves?*—1. A peculiar importance of matter. 2. A remarkable majesty and elevation of style. 3. Purity of doctrine. 4. Mutual agreement of all parts. 5. The design of the who e, which is to render all glory to God. 6. Light and power to convince and convert sinners; and to comfort and build up believers unto salvation. (Conf. Faith, 1: 5.

These evidences of Divine Inspiration are found only in the Scriptures of the Old and New Testaments. (*Append. Note, E.*)

THE BIBLE—ITS HISTORY.

In what part of the world was the Bible written?—At different places in the south-western part of Asia, and in the south-eastern part of Europe.

Were all the Books of the Bible written at one time?— They were not: GENSIS, the first Book, was written by Moses nearly 1,500 years before the advent of Christ; and the REVELATION, the last, by the Apostle John, about 97 or 98 years after Christ.

The other Books were written by the persons whose names they respectively bear, at different times between those dates.

In what languages were the Scriptures originally written?—The Old Testament was written in Hebrew, (with the exception of a part of the Book of Daniel, which is in Chaldee,) and the New Testament, in Greek.

Why was the Old Testament written in Hebrew, and the New Testament in Greek?—Because Hebrew was the language of the Jews, to whom the Old Testament was committed, (Rom. 3: 1, 2.) And Greek was the most popular language of the civilized world at the introduction of the Gospel, which was designed for the world at large.

When were the Books of the Bible collected and arranged in their present order?—(1.) In the reign of Artaxerxes I. King of Persia, (B. C. 457,) Ezra the Scribe, returned from Babylon to Jerusalem, and among other important works, he collected and arranged the Books of the Old Testament, adding to the number then extant, the two Books of Chronicles, the 1st, and 119th Psalms, and the Historical Book which bears his name.

(2.) During the lifetime of the Apostle John, who wrote a Gospel, three Epistles, and the Revelation, all the Books of the New Testament, together with those of the Old Testament, were received and acknowleged by the churches as Holy Inspired Scripture.

(3.) During the second and third centuries, Clement, Irenæus. and Tertullian, speak of the New Testament as consisting of two parts: GOSPELS and EPISTLES. And in the fourth century, (A. D. 360,) the Synod of Laodicea, separated the genuine Books of the New Testament, from the many spurious or apocrypha! writings, that had been published in the name of the Apostles; and from the genuine, though uninspired productions of the early period of the Gospel.

When was the Bible first translated into any other language?—In the year B. C. 277, the Old Testament was translated into Greek, at Alexandria, by order of Ptolemy Philadelphus, king of Egypt. This translation, from the seventy-two learned men by whom it was made, is named THE SEPTUAGINT, (*Septuaginta, seventy.*) These learned men, six representing

each of the twelve tribes of Israel, were for this purpose sent from Jerusalem, by Eleazer, the High Priest,
at the request of the king of Egypt.

*What other important translations were made at an
early period of the Church?*—The Gospel having been
preached and churches planted in almost every part
of the world, by the Apostles and early Evangelists,
the Scriptures, were, at an early period, translated
into various languages for the use of the several
churches. Among those translations may be mentioned the Syriac, Arabic, Persian, Egyptian or Cop-
tic, Ethiopian, Sclavonic or old Russian. The Italic
or Latin, the Gothic, and the Anglo-Saxon. Manu-
script copies of these ancient translations are still in
existence.

Dr. Claudius Buchannan, in the year, A. D. 1807,
found in the possession of the Syrian churches on the
western coast of India, very ancient copies of the
Syriac Bible. Those churches were in the first
instance, gathered and established by the missionary
labors of the Apostle Thomas.

*When was the Vulgate or Common Latin Translation
of the Bible made?*—In the latter part of the fourth
century, (A. D. 384,) by Jerome, a learned monk of
Palestine. This translation, although frequently cor-
rected by the authority of different Popes, is still, in
many passages, quite erroneous. It has, nevertheless
been adopted by the Church of Rome as their authentic version of the Holy Scriptures, instead of the inspired original Hebrew and Greek.

*What is the history of the English Bible prior to the
time of King James I.?*—Although we do not know the
precise date of the introduction of Christianity into
Britain, nor when the Holy Scriptures were first
translated into the language of the inhabitants, yet
there is reliable evidence, that for many hundred years

they possessed parts at least, of the Word of God, in their vernacular tongue.

After the Saxon translations of the whole Bible or of particular Books, made by Adhelm, bishop of Sherborn, 706; by Egbert, bishop of Lindisfern, 706; by the venerable Bede, 735; by the illustrious king Alfred, 870; and by Elfred, Archbishop of Canterbury, 995; the first English translation was made by an unknown person about the year 1290; and the next, by the celebrated John Wiclif in 1380. But those translations were never printed.

The first printed English translation of the Scriptures was accomplished by the Martyr, William Tyndale, in 1526, at Atwerp, whither he had retired to prosecute his work in safety from Henry VIII. In the year 1535, Miles Coverdale, a man eminent for piety and learning, printed and published the whole Bible, which he had translated into English. In 1560, (Elizabeth,) a number of pious and learned English ministers, who had taken refuge at Geneva from persecution at home, published the whole Bible which they had carefully translated into English. This is called "THE GENEVA BIBLE."

In 1568, Abp. Parker completed THE GREAT BIBLE, or as it is usually named THE BISHOPS' BIBLE, from the circumstance, that eight of the persons employed in the translation were bishops.

What opposition was made to these efforts to supply the People, with the Word of God in their own language? — The Church of Rome teaching that the Bible was intended for the clergy and not for the people, had, from the time of Pope Gregory IX, (A. D. 1229,) strictly forbidden the laity to read the Holy Scriptures without the license of a bishop. Accordingly the labors of the Reformers in translating and publishing the Word of God for the use of the people generally, subjected them to the severest persecution.

In the reign of Henry IV., king of England, Arundel, Archbishop of Canterbury, caused several persons to be burned for having read the New Testament and the Ten Commandments in Wiclif's Translation. Henry V. caused a law to be enacted, that
"whoever read the Scriptures in their mother tongue,
should forfeit land, cattle, body, life, and goods from
their heirs for ever; and be condemned for heretics to
God, enemies to the crown, and most arrant traitors
to the land."

When Tyndale's translation of the New Testament
first appeared in England, in the reign of Henry VIII.
Tonstal, Bishop of London and Sir Thomas More
bought up almost the whole edition, and burned it at
St. Paul's Cross. This, however, enabled Tyndale to
print a larger edition, which was issued in 1534. But
the importers and venders of these copies, were condemned by Sir Thomas More, to ride with their faces
to the horses' tails, with paper caps upon their heads,
and with copies of the New Testament tied about
them; which, when they reached the standard in
Cheapside, they were compelled to throw into a great
fire. They were then fined a considerable sum of
money. At length, Tyndale, at the instigation of
Henry VIII. was seized and thrown into prison in
Flanders, where, in 1536, he was strangled and burned.
The same fate afterwards attended Tyndale's two
devoted assistants, John Fry and William Roye.

After king Henry VIII. had thrown off the authority of the Pope of Rome, and had placed himself at
the head of the Church of England, 1534, he yielded
to the solicitation of Archbishop Cranmer and other
friends of the Reformation, to have the Word of God
given to the people. And as the printing of the
Bible could then be executed better at Paris than
in England, Henry obtained for his printers, permission from the King of France, to print it in that city.

But, notwithstanding this royal license, the Inquisition issued an order for the arrest of the French printers, their English employers, Grafton and Whitechurch, and Coverdale, the corrector of the work; while they seized and condemned to the flames, 2,500 copies of the work! (Dec. 17th, 1538.)

But notwithstanding all this opposition, the precious Word of God has come to us *in our own language,* a faithful version of the Inspired Originals; albeit baptized with the Blood of martyred Translators, Printers, and Bible Readers.

When was the English Bible now in general use, published?—In the year 1611, by the authority of James I. King of England. From this circumstance, this translation is frequently called King James' Bible.

In how many languages is the Bible now printed and published?—In nearly two hundred, chiefly by the agency of The British and Foreign Bible Society, formed in 1804; and of The American Bible Society, established in 1816.

THE BIBLE—ITS DIVISIONS.

1. *Of what two chief parts does the Bible consist?*—Of the Old Testament and the New Testament.

2. *Why is the first part called The Old Testament?*—Because it records the Institutions, Promises and Threatenings, of the several Dispensations of the true Religion, which were first given to man.

3. *Why is the second part called The New Testament?* Because it records the introduction of the later Dispensation or Covenant, in the personal ministry of the Lord Jesus Christ.

4. *What is the relation of the Two Testaments to each other?*—The Old Testament foreshows Christ *to come*, and the nature of his Salvation, in Types, Symbols, Ceremonies, and Prophecies; and The New Testament shows that all things thus foretold of Christ, were fulfilled in the Person and Work of Jesus of Nazareth.

5. *What is meant by a Dispensation of Religion?*—So much of the Divine Will as it has pleased God to reveal at any one time.

6. *How many such Dispensations have been given?*—Five: 1. The Adamic. 2. The Noachian. 3. The Abrahamic. 4. The Mosaic. 5. The Christian. Of these, four are recorded in the Old Testament, and one in the New Testament; while both Testaments predict a sixth Dispensation, which will be The Millenium.

7. *How many Books are there in the Old Testament?* Thirty-nine.

8. *How many Books are there in the New Testament?* Twenty-seven, in all Sixty-six.

9. *How may the Books of The Old Testament be classified?*—In three classes: thus, 17 Historical, (Gen. Est.;) 6 Poetical, (Job, Cant., Lam.;) 16 Prophetical, (Isa., Lam., Mal.)

10. *How may the Books of The New Testament be arranged?*—In three classes, also, thus: 5 Historical, (Matt., Acts.;) 21 Epistolary, (Rom.,—Jude;) 1 Prophetical, (Revelation.)

```
                                 ⎧ 17  Historical.
                    ⎧ Old Test. ⎪
                    ⎪           ⎨  6  Poetical.
                    ⎪ 39 Books. ⎪
                    ⎪           ⎩ 16  Prophetical.
                    ⎪
  Holy Bible,       ⎪
                    ⎨
  66 Books.         ⎪
                    ⎪
                    ⎪           ⎧  5  Historical.
                    ⎪ N.  Test. ⎪
                    ⎪           ⎨ 21  Epistolary.
                    ⎩ 27 Books. ⎪
                                ⎩  1  Prophetical.
```

11. *How are the several Books of the Bible divided?*—Into Chapters and Verses.

12. *When and why was this division made?*—It was made about the year 1651 A. D., for convenience in finding particular passages.

13. *How many Chapters in the Old Testament?*—929.

14. *How many Chapters in the New Testament?*—270. In the whole Bible, 1,199.

15. *How many Verses in the Old Testiment?*—23,214.

16. *How many Verses in the New Testament?*—7,959. In the whole Bible, 31,173.

17. *How many Chapters must be read daily in order to read the Bible through in a year?*—Three every week day ; and five every Sabbath day.

THE DESIGN OF THE BIBLE.

1. *For what purpose was the Bible given to us?*—To teach us what we are to believe concerning God, and what duty God requires of us.

2. *How is the Bible adapted to this purpose?*—Besides being divinely Inspired, (see Revealed Rel., Sec. 1, Quest. 1—11.) it is 1. Sufficient, revealing all needful faith and duty. 2. It is Perspicuous to the common mind. 3. Its decisions are Authoritative, being supreme and final. 4. Its authority is independent of human testimony.

3. *How does it appear that the Bible is a perfect rule of faith and duty?*—1. Because it is able to make a child wise unto salvation through faith in Jesus Christ; and to furnish the man of God thoroughly unto all good works. (2 Tim. 3: 15, 16, 17 ; Ps. 119: 9.)

2. Because we are forbidden in the most solemn manner, either to add to the Word of God, or to take anything from it. (Prov. 30: 6; Rev. 22: 18, 19; Deut. 4: 2; Gal. 1: 8.)

4. *How may it be proved that the Scriptures are perspicuous, or easily understood by people generally?*—1. By such texts as these: Ps. 19: 8; 119: 130; Prov. 30: 5 ; 2 Tim. 3: 15, which either directly assert or necessarily imply the perspicuity of the Scriptures.

2. By those texts which invite general attention to the Scriptures, or command personal investigation of their teachings: such as, Isa. 34: 1, 16; Jno. 5: 39; Acts. 17: 11; Eph. 6: 17; Col. 3: 16; Deut. 6: 7, 9; 1 Thess. 5: 21; 1 Jno. 4: 1; 1 Cor. 10: 15; 1 Peter, 3: 15; 2 Peter, 1: 16, 21.

5. *Are all parts of the Scriptures easily understood?*–No, they are not, (2 Peter 3: 16,) "yet those things which are necessary to be known, believed, and observed for salvation, are so clearly propounded in some place of

Scripture or other, that not only the learned, but the unlearned, in a due use of the ordinary means, may attain unto a sufficient understanding of them." (2 Tim. 3: 15; Ps. 1: 1, 2; 19: 7; Rev. 1: 3; Jno. 5: 39, 46; Acts 15: 15; Ps: 119: 105.)

6. *What texts prove that in deciding all questions in religion and morals, we are to rest finally in the teaching of the Bible?*—(Matt. 22: 29, 31; Eph. 2: 20; Acts 28: 25; Isa 8: 20; Luke 24: 27.)

7. *Whence do the Holy Scriptures derive their supreme authority as the perfect and final rule of our faith and life?*—Not from the testimony of any man, or council, or assembly, or church; but wholly from the inward work of the Holy Spirit the author of the Scriptures, bearing witness by, and with, the Word in our hearts. (John 6: 45; 16: 13, 14; 1 Cor. 2: 10, 12; 1 Thess. 2: 13; 1 John 2: 20, 27; 5: 9.) Con. F. 1: 7, 10.

OBJECTIONS TO THE BIBLE—Deists.

1. *By whom is the Bible especially rejected as the only sufficient rule of religious faith and practice?*—By the Deists, Jews, Mahometans, and the Church of Rome.

2. *What is the origin of the name Deist?*—It is from the Latin, *Deus*—God; and is given to one who professes to believe in God, and to worship him according to the light of nature; but who denies the divine inspiration and authority of the Holy Scriptures.

3. *By whom was the name Deist, first assumed?*—By a number of persons in France and Italy, in the sixteenth century, who desired to cover their opposition to the Christian religion, by a less objectionable name than that of *Atheist*. The first author by whom they are mentioned, is Viret, a reformer and divine, in 1563. The principles of deism, however, had existed from the earliest times.

4. *Who appears to have been the first deist?*—Cain, whose offering of the fruits of the earth, evidently acknowledged the existence of God, and his providential goodness; but in not offering a *Bleeding Sacrifice*, he evidently rejected the atonement to be made by the promised Redeemer, and denied the guilt of sin, both original and actual, which rendered that atonement necessary.

5. *Which are the chief points of deism, as held in modern times?*—Deism consists chiefly, 1. in the rejection of the Bible, especially with respect to its plenary inspiration, and the revealed truth concerning the redemption of sinners by the atonement of the Son of God. 2. In a professed belief in the existence of God, the Creator and Lawgiver of men. Deists are extravagant in their encomiums of natural religion; though they differ among themselves in regard to its moral obligations; and also, respecting a future state; some entirely denying that important doctrine.

6. *Who have been remarkable for their advocacy of deistical principles?*—Lord Herbert of Cherbury, Lord Bolingbroke, Voltaire, Volney, Rousseau, Diderot, Condorcet, Hume, Gibbon, Paine, and others of less note, but of equal hostility to the truth.

7. *What may be observed of the opposition of these writers to the Christian religion?*—That their objections do not so much refer to the religion of the Bible, as to the corruptions and superstitions of Romanism and other priest-craft. Such men as Paine, Bolingbroke, and Voltaire, must have been aware, that in confounding the errors and puerilities of Romanism, with the pure and sublime teachings of the Gospel, they were committing the greatest injustice. Yet judging from some of the writings of these noted infidels, it is very doubtful that they ever read the Bible through.

8. *By whom have the principles of deism been ably refuted?*—By Watson, Bishop of Llandaff, in a masterly treatise, entitled, "AN APOLOGY FOR THE BIBLE." By Dr. Beattie in his "ESSAY ON TRUTH." By Leland, in his "VIEW OF DEISTICAL WRITERS." By Faber, in his "DIFFICULTIES OF INFIDELITY." By Leslie, in his "SHORT AND EASY METHOD WITH THE DEISTS." And by the late Rev. David Nelson, M. D., in his "CAUSE AND CURE OF INFIDELITY."

9. *What practical arguments may be adduced against the system of deism, or natural religion?*—1. So far as there is any truth in natural religion, it was designed for man in a state of innocency; and therefore it does not provide a "Saviour of Sinners." (1 Cor. 1: 21, 23.) 2. As a Rule of Life, it is insufficient and inoperative, in consequence of the extreme corruption and depravity of fallen human nature. (Rom. 1: 18, 32.) 3. No one has ever been made either a better or happier man by disbelieving the Bible. (Ps. 1: 1, 2; 119: 9.) 4. If, as the deists assert, the Prophets and Apostles were not divinely inspired, then they must have been more than mere mortal men; because they had either superhuman knowledge to be able to foretell events, hundreds of years before those events transpired; or else, they exercised superhuman power in bringing to pass the accomplishment of their own predictions, hundreds of years after they were dead. 5. Again, since the sacred writers expressly assert, that they spoke by the authority of God, and as they were moved by the Spirit of God; if the deists are correct in denying this, the Prophets and Apostles were the most wicked and foolish of men. For they were guilty of falsehood and blasphemy in publishing as *The Word of God, a cunning fable devised by themselves!* And impious liars as they must be, if the deists are right; their folly is unaccountable, in

bringing upon themselves all trouble, and even death itself, by preaching a doctrine designed to make all other men wise and virtuous. And thus, deism, in rejecting the Bible as the INSPIRED WORD OF GOD, requires a degree of faith, which amounts to presumptuous and senseless credulity.

10. *How may we prove in opposition to deism, the historic truth of the miracles and other facts recorded in the Scriptures?*—1. The miracles and other matters of fact in the Scripture history, were so peculiarly exposed and subject to men's outward senses of seeing and hearing, that they could not have been deceived respecting them. 2. They occured publicly, in the face of the world; they "were not done in a corner." 2. The Scripture narrative is not a verbal tradition written and published long after the original parties had passed away. But on the contrary, it was for the most part, recorded and published in the life time of the original witnesses; who could easily have contradicted the account, had it been a falsehood. But no such contradiction was ever made, even by the most embittered foes. 4. The great essential facts recorded in both the Old and New Testaments, have been commemorated from time immemorial, by the observance of certain rites and ceremonies, which were instituted at the time for this purpose. Such as the observance of the seventh day of the week, in commemoration of the Creation of all things in six days, and God's resting the seventh day. The rite of Circumcision, still practiced by the descendants of Abraham, in testimony of God's covenant with that patriarch. The national observance of the Passover by the Jews, in commemoration of their deliverance from the land of Egypt. The celebration of the Lord's Supper, in testimony of Christ's sacrificial death. The observance of the first day of the week, in commemoration of Christ's resurrection from the

dead. And the practice of admitting converts to the Christian Church by the ordinance of Baptism, in obedience to the command of Christ, and in virtue of his supreme authority.

If the Scripture account of the origin of these venerable observances, is not the truth; it is manifestly incumbent on all that reject the testimony of the Holy Scriptures on these points, to show when, why, and by whom, these institutions were introduced.

Opposition of the Jews.

11. *Who are the Jews?*—The descendants of Abraham, Isaac and Jacob; according to the promise of God, (Gen. 12: 7; 17: 19; 27: 29; 28: 10—15; Rom. 9: 7—13.) They were the chosen depositaries of the Word of God and the true religion, for nearly 2,000 years, (B. C. 1921—A. D. 70; Rom. 3: 1, 2.) For their rejection of Jesus, the promised Messiah, they have been deprived of their peculiar privileges. Their city and temple, were captured and destroyed by the Romans, after an obstinate siege of nearly six months, during which, more than a million of persons perished. (A. D. 70.) The captives were sold into bondage, or otherwise scattered over the earth; yet are they preserved from age to age, a distinct people; and so to remain until the times of the Gentiles be fulfilled. (Rom. chap, 11.)

12. *What objection do the Jews urge against the Holy Scriptures?*—While they professedly receive the Old Testament as the Inspired Word of God, and the authentic record of their ancient national history; yet, rejecting the claim of Jesus to the Messiahship, they, of course, reject the New Testament as uninspired, and forming no part of the Word of God; since this Testament records the evidences that Jesus of Nazareth is the Messiah, the Son of God, and the Saviour of men.

13. *What do the Jews profess to believe concerning Jesus?*—That he was a man of superior genius, falsely claiming to be the Messiah. And while the ancient Jews attributed his miracles to the influence of Satan; their descendants to the present day, with no less folly and blasphemy, say, that his miracles were wrought by the power of magic arts, which he learned in Egypt. The same opinion was entertained by Celsus, Julian the Apostate, and other ancient heathen adversaries; and it is held also, by many deists of the present day.

14. *How did our Saviour meet and rebuke the malicious assertion, which attributed his miracles to the power of Satan?*—Matt. chap. 12 : 22—37.

15. *Whence appears the unreasonableness of attributing the miracles of Jesus to magic?*—From the insufficiency of magic to accomplish the works wrought by the blessed Redeemer. No magic arts ever known or practised by man, no necromancy, nor any Satanic influence, have ever been able to accomplish a single miracle. (*Append. Note F.*)

It is therefore, weak and unreasonable in the last degree, to assign the miracles of Jesus, the most holy, benignant, and wonderful works ever accomplished on earth, to an agency which has never effected any thing more than mere deceptive slight-of-hand juggles; and never practised by any but wicked and designing men, who for the crime of counterfeiting miracles by magic, were by the Mosaic Law, condemned to death. (Exod. 22 : 18; Lev. 20 : 27.)

16. *What was the conviction of the many competent and unprejudiced witnesses, who repeatedly beheld the divine works of our blessed Redeemer?*—That which must be the full persuation of every intelligent man, fairly open to conviction, when placed in those circumstances. (John 3 : 1, 3; 6 : 14; 9 : 33; 10 : 20, 21; 11 : 47.)

17. *What is to be inferred from the fact, that such men as Nicodemus, Saul, Joseph of Arimathea, Barnabus, and a great company of the Priests, who, at the sacrifice of all earthly interests, became obedient to the faith of Christ?*—That as they were all persons of intelligence, education, or distinction, and enjoying the best possible opportunity of forming a correct judgment respecting the miracles of Jesus, their profession of faith in Christ, affords the strongest evidence that they regarded the miracles of the Redeemer, as real transactions, and wrought by the power of God. (Acts 1: 15; 2: 41; 4: 4, and chapters 5, 6.)

18. *What may also be observed respecting the conversion of those heathen lawyers and philosophers, such as Clemens Romanus, Justin Martyr, Clement of Alexandria, Tertulian, and Cyprian, who after the times of the Apostles, and during the Roman Persecutions, renounced their heathenism and embraced the Gospel?*—That as they were peculiarly well qualified to examine all the questions involved, their acceptance of Christ as he was offered to them in the Gospel, affords the clearest evidence, that the record of the miracles and other divine testimonies to the mission of Christ, had lost none of their authenticity with the lapse of time.

19. *What motives influenced the Jewish Rulers in rejecting the claims of Jesus to the Missiahship?*—The fear of losing their wealth and authority; and in their bitter hostility to the Son of God, they fulfilled their own Scriptures in condemning him. (John 11: 47, 48; Acts 13: 27.)

20. *Whence proceeded the hostility of the unbelieving Jews, to Jesus, as claiming to be their long promised Missiah or Christ?*—1. From their great personal and national corruption.

2. From their erroneous views of the prophecies of the Messiah, and the nature of his kingdom. They

looked for a temporal Prince to deliver them from their political foes, and not for a spiritual Redeemer to save them from their sins.

3. The Ru ers and chief men hated Christ because he exposed and rebuked their vices, their pride, and their hypocrisy.

4. They feared that the growing popularity of Jesus with the common people, would either directly destroy their authority in the nation; or furnish occasion to the Romans to come and complete their subjugation.

5. Having accomplished Christ's death, and being seriously and justly alarmed at the undeniable evidences of his resurrection; they felt bound in justice to themselves, to oppose, and if possible, suppress the truth, by the persecution of his disciples.

6. The modern Jews, to a great extent, under the influence of the same principles and prejudices, have continued in the same opposition to the Redeemer; and have thus perpetuated the calamities, which, as divine judgments, the Prophets foretold should come upon them, if they rejected their anointed king, Messiah, the Prince. (Deut. 18: 15—19; Isa. 6: 8—12, compared with John 12: 37—41; Rom. 11: 8—10.)

JESUS OF NAZARETH,
The Messiah of the Old Testament.

21. *What chief particulars respecting the Messiah, were foretold by the Old Testament Prophets, and which were fulfilled in the person of Jesus of Nazareth?*—1. His family descent, and his divinity.

2. The circumstances of his birth.

3. The official character of his life.

4. His ignominious and cruel death, and his honorable burial.

5. His resurrection and ascention to heaven.

22. *From what family was it foretold the Messiah should be descended?*—From Abraham, in the line of Isaac, Jacob, Judah, and king David. (Gen. 12: 3; 26: 4; 28: 14; 49: 10; 17: 19; 21: 12; 27: 29; 46: 12; Ruth, 4: 18—22; Psalm, 132: 11—18; Isa. 11: 1; Jer. 23: 5—6.)

23. *Where do we find recorded the fulfilment of these predictions in the person of Jesus?*—In Matthew, 1: 1—17; and Luke, 3: 23—38.

24. *How may we explain the differences which occur between the account of the lineage of Jesus as given by the Evangelist Matthew, and that given by the Evangelist Luke?*—The design of Matthew evidently is to establish the claim of Jesus to the throne of David, as the heir of his *reputed or legal* father, Joseph, who was descended from Solomon, David's successor on the throne, (Matt. 1: 6.) Whereas Luke intends to prove the validity of the Saviour's title to the throne in right of his mother Mary, who was the daughter of Heli, a descendant of David, through Nathan, his elder son. (Luke, 3: 31.) And thus it appears from the united testimony of Matthew and Luke, that the only two branches of descent from king David, one through his elder son, Nathan, and the other through his yougest son and successor, Solomon, uniting in Joseph and Mary, all natural and legal right to the throne of David, centered and terminated in Jesus Christ.

Joseph was the real son of Jacob, (Matt. 1: 16,) and although not the natural father of Jesus; yet according to the method of keeping Jewish family registers, his name is placed in the genealogy. But having espoused Mary, he is, as her husband, named by Luke the son of her father, Heli, (Luke, 3: 23.) Other points of apparent disagreement between Matthew and Luke in the genealogy of Christ, are satisfactorily explained in the Commentaries.

25. *What was foretold by the Prophets respecting the personal nature of the Messiah?*—That he would be both God and man, possessing two distinct natures in one person, for ever. (Psalm, 2: 7; 110: 1; Isa, 9: 6; Micah, 5: 2; Isa. 6: 1—12, with John, 12: 37-41.)

26. *How were these predictions fulfilled in the person of Jesus of Nazareth?*—Heb. chap. 1; Matt. 22: 41—46; John, 1: 1—3, 14; Rom. 9: 5; 1 Cor. 15: 24, 25; Gal. 4: 4, 5.

27. *What particulars were foretold by the Prophets respecting the Nativity of the Messiah, and which were fulfilled in the experience of Jesus?*—1. That he was to be born of a Virgin. (Isa. 7: 14; Matt. 1: 21—23.)

2. At Bethlehem. (Micah, 5: 2; Matt. 2: 1—6; Luke, 2: 4—14; John, 7: 42.)

3. That a Star should appear at his birth. (Numb. 24: 17; Isa. 60: 3; Matt. 2: 2—10; Luke, 1: 78; 2 Peter, 1: 19; Rev. 22: 16.

4. That the time of Christ's advent, would be in connection with the final loss of national sovereignty by the Jewish people. (Gen. 49: 10; Matt. 2: 1; Luke 2: 1, 3.) After the advent of Christ, the Jews never regained their national independence. For some time after the death of Herod the Great, his dominions were governed by his sons, as Tetrarchs under the authority of the Roman Emperor. Then reduced to a province, Judea was governed by Roman Procurators; one of whom, Pontius Pilate, in the reign of the Emperor Tiberius, authorized the crucifixion of our Lord. And finally, the whole Jewish state was subverted and abolished by Titus, the son of the Emperor Vespasian, A. D. 70. Truly the Sceptre departed from Judah, for Shiloh was come,

according to the prediction of the Patriarch. (Gen. 49: 10.)

28. *What particulars are foretold respecting the official work of Christ, and which were fulfilled by Jesus?*— 1. That he was to be a Prophet; (Deut. 18: 15—18; with Matt. 17: 5; Luke, 7: 16; 24: 19; John 6: 14.)

2. That he was to be a Priest; (Psalm, 110: 4; with Heb. 6: 20; Isa. 53: 4—12; with 2 Cor. 5: 21; Isa. 61: 1—3; with Luke, 4: 16—21; John, 4: 25, 26; Heb. 2: 17; 4: 14; 9: 14. Zech. 6: 13; with Matt. 26: 61—64; John, 1: 29.)

3. That he was to be a King; (Psalm, 2: 6; 132: 11; with John, 18: 32—37; Luke, 19: 37, 38.)

29. *What was predicted respecting the miraculous power of Christ?*—Isa. 35: 3—6; 42: 5—9.

30. *In what instances were these predictions fulfilled by Jesus?*—Matt. 4: 23, 24; 11: 1—6; 15: 29—39; 19: 2.

31. *What was foretold respecting the treatment which the Messiah would receive from the Jews?*—That he would be despised and rejected by the nation generally; and that he would be betrayed and sold for thirty pieces of silver, by one of his disciples, (Isa. 53: 1—3; Psalm, 41: 9; 55: 12—14; Zech, 11: 12, 13.)

32. *Where do we find the record of the accomplishment of these predictions, in the experience of Jesus?*—John, 1: 11; 8: 49; Matt. 26: 1—5, 14—25; 27: 3—10, 20—26.

33. *What was foretold by the Prophets respecting the circumstances that would attend the sacrificial death of the Messiah?*—Psalm, 22: 7, 8, 16, 17, 18; 34: 20; 69: 21; Isa, 50: 6; 53: 5, 8, 12; Zech. 12: 10; 13: 6.

34. *How were these predictions fulfilled in the person of Jesus the Son of Mary?*—Matt. 27: 39—43—48, 49; John, 19: 1—3, 17, 18, 23, 24, 29, 31—37.

35. *W..ut was foretold respecting the burial of Christ; and how was it fulfilled in the person of Jesus?*—That although he was numbered with transgressors, and his grave appointed with the wicked; yet his burial place should actually be with the rich. (Isa. 53:9; with Matt. 27: 38, 57—60.)

36. *What was foretold respecting the resurrection of Christ; and which was fulfilled in the experience of Jesus?*—Psalm, 16: 9, 10; Isa. 53: 10; John 2: 19—21; 10: 17; Mark, 10: 34; with Matt. 28: 5, 6. Acts 2: 31, 32; 13: 26—41; 1 Cor. 15: 4—20.

37. *What was predicted respecting the ascension of Christ?*—Psalm, 68: 18; which prophecy was fulfilled in the event recorded, Mark, 16: 19; Luke, 24: 50, 51; Acts, 1: 9.

38. *What may be observed respecting the fulfillment of the prediction: "Thou hast led captivity captive?"*—That it began immediately after the resurrection of Jesus, in the resurrection of those "saints that appeared unto many;" and who, as the first fruits of victory, were led home in triumph by the ascending Redeemer, in testimony of the complete salvation of all his people from sin, death, the grave, and hell. Matt. 27: 52, 53; 1sa. 26: 19; 1 Cor. 15: 55—57.)

39. *What remarkable prophecy of the Old Testament determines the exact time when Christ must come for the redemption of his people?*—The Prophecy of Daniel, (chap. 9: 20—27.) in which it is foretold that Christ, the Messiah, would appear and put away sin by the sacrifice of himself, at the expiration of "Seventy-Weeks," (of years,) that is 490 years, counted from the year, B. C. 457, when Ezra was commissioned to return to Jerusalem, by Artaxerxes, king of Persia, in the seventh year of his reign, and on the first day of the month *Nisan*, which was the first month of the Jewish sacred year. (Ezra, chap. 7th.)

40. *When did these Seventy Weeks terminate?*—In A. D. 33; (B. C. 457—A.D. 33=490;) when Messiah the Prince, Christ Jesus, was crucified at Jerusalem, on the day before the Passover, which occurred on the first day of the month *Nisan.*

41. *How does the Prophecy divide this remarkable period of Seventy Weeks?*—Into three minor periods: 1st. "Seven Weeks," 49 years, for the restoration of Jerusalem, which expired with Nehemiah's last act of reformation, B. C. 408. 2d. "Sixty-two Weeks," 434 years, from Nehemiah, to the announcement of Christ by John the Baptist, A. D. 26. 3d. "One Week," 7 years, for the joint personal ministry of John the Baptist and of Jesus; each three years and a half, from A. D. 26, to A. D. 33, when by the vicarious death of the Son of God, all other sacrifices for sin, were for ever abolished, and "an everlasting righteousness brought in."

42. *What must be inferred from this intimate relation between the prophecies of the Old Testament and the history of the New Testament, respecting Christ?*—Without the prophecies of the Old Testament, we should not have known that Christ ever intended to come and save sinners; and without the history of the New Testament, we should not know that he had come and redeemed his people, according to his promise.

43. *To what dilemma are the Jews reduced, by the consideration of these prophecies respecting the Messiah, which were so evidently fulfilled in the person and life of Jesus of Nazareth?*—Either, that JESUS OF NAZARETH IS THE TRUE MESSIAH; or that THE WORD OF GOD BY HIS PROPHETS HAS UTTERLY FAILED!

Mahometan Objections.

44. *Who are the Mahometans?*—The followers of Mahomet, the founder of a false religion, who began to propagate his system at Mecca, in Arabia, about the year A. D. 612.

45. *What is the character of the Mahomatan religion?* The religion of Mahomet, which is contained in the KORAN, is a compound of Paganism, Judaism, and Deism. Its chief tenet is: "There is but one God, and Mahomet is his prophet." Adapted to the base and ambitious passions of men, and propagated by the force of arms, it rapidly spread through Arabia, Syria, India, Africa; and, but for the defeat of the Saracen army by Charles Martel, in the battle of Tours, (A. D. 732,) the religion of the false prophet would have supp[l]anted the liberties and the religion of Western Europe.

46. *What objections do the Mahometans urge against the Bible?*—The Mahometans, tracing their descent as Arabs, from Ishmael, the eldest son of Abraham, admit, for the most part, the Scripture history of Abraham and the other patriarchs; and they do not deny that Jesus Christ was a true Prophet. But they insist, that the mission of Jesus, like that of Moses, was to be temporary, and was to be succeeded by that of Mahomet, who, they pretend, was the Comforter promised by Christ, (John, 16: 7.) But in as much, as the Bible teaches, that the Comforter promised by Christ, is THE HOLY GHOST, (John, 14: 16, 17;) that Jesus, himself, is a Priest and King for ever, and one with the Father and the Holy Spirit—that Jesus is the only Head of his redeemed Church—that the claims of Jesus to the love and adoration of men, admit of no compromise nor concession; the Mahometans reject the Bible in bitter hostility to its divine Author, and to all that love his precious name.

47. *How do the claims of Mahomet to be a true prophet
compare with those of the Apostles of Christ?*—It is
expressly declared by Christ that his Apostles should
not die by poison, (Mark, 16: 18.) and there is neither
record nor tradition, that any of them died by that
means. But Mahomet, who styled himself "The
Prophet of God," lost his life by poison. Undoubtedly, had he been a true prophet or apostle of God, he
would not have fallen into the snare of eating the
meat, which had been poisoned to destroy him.

48. *What practical objection to Mahometanism, is
found in the system itself?*—One of the duties imperatively enjoined on its disciples, is to observe The Ramadan, during which, no food or drink may be taken
from sun rise to sun set: an utter impossibility in
those parts of the world where there is but one day
and one night in the whole year. Mahometanism,
therefore, unlike the Gospel of Christ, cannot be
preached and received "in all the world." [*Append. G.*]

Opposition of Rome.

1. *What is the Church of Rome?*—It is that ecclesiastical body which submits to the authority of the
Pope of Rome, as the successor of Peter and Vicar
of Christ.

2. *Where do we find the authentic statement of the doctrines of the papal community.*—In the Catechism and
Decrees of the Council of Trent; in the Creed of
Pope Pius IV., and in other publications authorized
by the Pope or any of the papal bishops.

3. *What does the Church of Rome teach respecting the
Holy Scriptures.*—Several doctrines quite at variance
with the generally received faith of the Church of
Christ upon this important subject: 1. That as the
revealed Word of God consists of two parts of equal

authority, the Written Word, called Holy Scripture, and the Unwritten Word, called Divine Tradition, therefore the Holy Scripture without Tradition, is not sufficient to make us wise unto salvation.

THE TRADITIONS OF ROMANISM.

4. *What does the Church of Rome mean by "Divine Traditions"?*—Those doctrines and observances of her religion, which, it is affirmed, were not recorded by inspired Prophets and Apostles, but which have been orally transmitted from age to age from the beginning.

5. *How does Rome attempt to illustrate and justify her doctrine of "Divine Tradition"?*—By affirming that the doctrines and duties of the Old Testament Dispensation, existed as traditions before they were written by Moses; and, in like manner, the doctrines of the New Testament, were traditions before they were committed to writing by the Evangelists.

6. *What may be replied to this statement?*—It is indeed true, that some of the early institutions of the true religion may have existed as traditions before they were written by Moses, such as the institution of the Sabbath, the offering of a bleeding sacrifice in testimony of faith in the promised Redeemer, and the rite of circumcision; but when Moses committed those divine ordinances to writing, they ceased to be oral traditions, and became of permanent written record. While with respect to the whole Levitical system, no part of it ever existed as an oral tradition; for it was, in all its details, committed to writing by Moses, as soon as he received it from the Lord, Jehovah, himself, writing the Ten Commandments on two Tables of Stone.

- In like manner, the doctrines and institutions of the Christian Church, never existed as traditions, in the papal sense; for they were who'ly committed to writing by inspired men, in the life time of the Apostles, who had received them from our blessed Lord himself.

7. *What doctrines and observances constitute the Traditions of the Church of Rome?*—Those of the Seven Sacraments, the Real Presence, Transubstantiation, Invoking the Saints, Purgatory, Praying for the Dead, &c.

8. *Is it not morally certain that these so-called "Divine Traditions" were invented by the Romish Clergy and received by the credulity of the people, long after the Holy Scriptures were written?*—Undoubtedly, and for the following reasons:

1st. Christianity was introduced into Britain at a very early period, probably in the days of the Apostles. But when Austin with forty monks, arrived in England as missionaries from Pope Gregory the Great, (A. D. 597,) the British Christians refused to adopt the new creed brought from Rome; because it differed essentially from the ancient Gospel, they had received from their ancestors. Twelve hundred of these original British Christian ministers, having assembled at Bangor, (A. D. 612,) spent three days in fasting and prayer, and still adhering to the truth which they had always held, they were attacked by the papal party which had been converted from among the pagan inhabitants, and all but fifty were massacred.

2d. When the Portuguese papal missionaries reached the coast of Malabar, south-western India, early in the sixteenth century, they found more than one hundred churches of Syrian Christians, whose pure and simple worship highly offended them. And when they asserted the sovereignty of the Pope over those churches, as the head of the universal church, the natives declared, "They did not know who the Pope of Rome was, and had never heard of him before." They further declared, "They had maintained the order and discipline of a regular Christian church, for more than thirteen hundred years, under the jurisdiction of the Patriarch of Antioch." "We," said they, "are of the true faith, whatever you of the West may be; for we came from the place where the followers of Christ were first called Christians." As soon as the Portuguese had become sufficiently powerful for their purpose, they established the Inquisition at Goa, and having invaded those tranquil churches, seized some of their clergy, and devoted them to the death of heretics. And having compelled many others to appear before a Synod, they accused them of the following practices and opinions: "That they had married wives; that they had only two sacraments, Baptism and the Lord's Supper; that they neither invoked saints, worshiped images, nor believed in Purgatory; and that they had no other orders or names of dignity in the church, than bishop, priest, and deacon."

These tenets they were called upon to abjure as heresies, or suffer suspension from all church benefices. (*Claudius Buchanan's Christian Researches in Asia, A. D.* 1807.)

3d. In the Catacombs of Rome, which were the secluded retreat of the early Christians for several hundred years during the pagan persecutions, there is not found a trace of any thing peculiar to the present Church of Rome. Among all the inscriptions and other mementoes of the original Christian faith, discovered in these homes of the living church, and of the bodies of their sainted dead, nothing is found to corroborate a single tradition of the present papal religion; not even the figure of a cross upon the tomb of a martyr. The only figure resembling a cross found in the Catacombs is that of the Greek letter X, the initial of the Greek word for Christ.

Most assuredly, if the peculiar dogmas of modern Romanism had been derived from our Lord Jesus Christ and his Apostles, as "divine traditions," all the early churches must have been familiar with them as constituting essential doctrines and rites of Christianity. But since the original churchs of Britain and India, had never known any thing of these unscriptural dogmas, until they were invaded by the emissaries of the Pope, it is evident, these dogmas must have been invented by the papists, after the planting of the Gospel of Christ in Britain and in India, and after the original Church in Rome itself, had emerged from her long refuge in the Catacombs.

9. *What is the authentic history of the rise of the Traditions of Romanism ?*—At an early period of the Church, the simple truths of the Gospel were corrupted by the gradual introduction of errors derived from the popular pagan philosophy; and those errors being entertained and countenanced by an ignorant or designing priesthood; and gaining strength among a still more ignorant populace, they were ultimately rendered obligatory in the estimation of all that submitted to the Bishop of Rome, by the decrees of Synods and Councils assembled by his authority. (*See Dualism*, and *Manes*, pp. 8, 9.)

1. The use of Holy Water, and the addition of Salt and Honey in the ordinance of Baptism arose in the second century.

2. Monastic Life originated in the third century; and in the fourth, the monks were formed into regular orders.

3. The Invocation of the Virgin Mary and of the Saints, introduced in the sixth century.

4. Papal Supremacy although claimed for a long time, was not definitely assumed and recognized until A. D. 606 in the person of Boniface III.

5. The Celibacy of the Clergy was enforced by Gregory VII., 1074.

6. The Immaculate Conception of Mary arose as a private opinion in 1140; in 1387 it became the subject of a fierce controversy; and was not promulgated as a *Divine Tradition* until 1854.

7. Transubstantiation was first definitely maintained by Pascasius Radbert, in 865; but it was not an authorized *Tradition* until it was so ordained by Innocent III., 1215.

8. The Laity were prohibited from reading the Scriptures by Gregory IX., 1229. (*Council of Toulouse.*)

9. That there are *Seven Sacraments*, and not only *two*, (as instituted by Christ,) was first definitely asserted in 1150; but this dogma did not become a *Tradition* until it was so decreed by the Council of Florence, 1439.

10. The dogma of Purgatory was derived from the Gnostic Philosophy. It was held as a speculation by Augustine, (400;) in the fifth century it became more definite and general; in the sixth, Pope Gregory made it practical, in connection with the Mass; and finally, the Councils of Ferrara and Florence, (1438, 9,) declared it a *Divine Tradition*.

11. Infallibility was for a long time claimed by the church; but for ages, nothing *authoritative*, was known concerning it. Some maintained, that the organ of Infallibility was the Pope; some, that it was a General Council; and others, that it resided in the Pope and a General Council, conjointly. Any opinion on the subject was allowed as lawful or probable, until 1870, when an Ecumenical Council decreed that Infallibility pertains to the Pope. And if any one

now, denies this *Divine Tradition*, "let him be accursed."

10. *Wherein consists the sin and danger of attempting to make Tradition a part of the Word of God?*—Prov. 30: 6; Rev. 22: 18, 19; Matt. 15: 1–9.

THE APOCRYPHA.

11. *Which is the second error of the Church of Rome, respecting the Holy Scriptures?*—The assertion that the Apocrypha is an essential part of the Written Word of God.

12. *What is the Apocrypha?*—The name APOCRYPHA, which literally signifies *hidden or concealed*, is given to certain ancient Jewish writings, which the Jews and Christians generally, have regarded as uninspired; or at most, of doubtful authority.

13. *What are the names of those apocryphal writings?* "The rest of the chapters of the Book of Esther;" "The Story of the Three Children;" "The Story of Susannah;" "The Story of Bel and the Dragon," added to the Book of Daniel;" The Books of "Tobit;" "Judith;" "Wisdom;" "Ecclesiasticus;" "Baruch," and the "Two Books of Maccabees."

14. *What is the judgment of the Church of Rome respecting these Books?*—The Council of Trent, which assembled in 1545, and whose decrees set forth the doctrines of the modern Church of Rome, declares, after enumerating the Apocrypha with the Inspired Books of the Old and New Testaments:—

"Whoever shall not receive as sacred and canonical. all these books, and every part of them, as they are read in the Catholic Church, and are contained in the Old Vulgate Latin edition, or shall knowingly and deliberately despise the aforesaid Traditions, let him be accursed." *Con. Trid. Dec. de Con. Scrip.*

15. *For what reasons do the Jews and the Church of*

Christ, exclude the Apocrypha from the canon of Inspired Scripture?—First. There is no evidence that the Apocrypha ever existed in Hebrew, the language in which "God spake unto the fathers by the Prophets," (Heb. 1: 1; Rom. 3: 1, 2.) On the contrary, the most ancient copies of the Apocrypha were either in Greek or Latin, languages not used by any Old Testament Prophet in recording the oracles of God.

Secondly. From the unquestioned testimony of authentic history, the apocryphal books above enumerated, were written between the time of the Prophet Malachi, (B. C. 400.) and that of John the Baptist, (A. D.) But during that period there arose no prophet among the Israelites: the prophetic spirit having been wholly withheld during that time. (Mal. 4: 4–6.) Accordingly, the Jewish Church never recognized the Apocrypha as a part of those inspired oracles of God, which had been by divine authority, committed to their custody. (Rom. 3: 1, 2.) And Josephus, the celebrated Jewish historian, who flourished in the first century of the Christian era, although writing a detailed account of the antiquities of his own people, their sacred books, &c., makes no mention whatever of these apocryphal writings, which the Church of Rome, nevertheless, declares, on her own authority, to be divinely inspired.

Thirdly. The Christian Church rejects the Apocrypha as uninspired, because our blessed Saviour and his Apostles, make no allusion to any part of these writings, while they quote numerous passages from the inspired books, which had been received as such by the Jewish Church, and which compose the present Old Testament of the Christian Church.

Fourthly. The writers of the Apocrypha do not claim to have been inspired. They do not, as Moses,

Samuel, David, Isaiah, and others, declare boldly and explicitly, that "The Lord said thus," or that "God spake all these words;" "Thus saith the Lord," &c. (Exod. 20: 1; Isa. 44: 1.) On the contrary, so far are they from asserting their own inspiration, that some of them say, what amounts to an acknowledgment, that they were not inspired. In the introduction to the Book of Ecclesiasticus, the writer entreats the reader "to pardon any errors he may have committed in *translating* the works of his grandfather into Greek."

In 1 Maccabees, 4th chapter, 46th verse, and 9th chapter, 27th verse, it is admitted that there was at that time, "no prophet in Israel." The second Book of Maccabes, (2: 23.) is an avowed abridgment of five books composed by Jason of Cyrene; and the author concludes with the following remark, which is utterly inconsistent with the idea that he was writing by inspiration: "If I have done well, and fitting the story, it is that which I desire; but if slenderly and meanly, it is that which I could attain unto." Such language is in marked contrast with the inspired words of the Lord's Prophets. Conscious of their high commission, and borne along by the Holy Spirit, they delivered their heavenly message, regardless of the praise or censure of men.

In the fifth place, the Apocrypha is unworthy a place among the canonical Scriptures, because in many instances, the writers contradict authentic history.

(1.) The author of the Book of Wisdom pretends that it was written by Solomon: a pretence evidently false, and bearing with it the proof, that the author, whoever he was, was not divinely inspired. He cites many passges from the prophecies of Isaiah and Jeremiah, which were not written until many ages

after the time of Solomon. Again, th's Book repre-
sents the Israelites as being in subjection to their
enemies, (Wis. 9: 7, 8, 15: 14,) whereas, we know
from t'1e Holy Scriptures, that the Israelites, during
the reign of Solomon, were eminently prosperous,
and in the enjoyment of great peace, were indepen-.
dent of all their enemies.

(2.) Baruch is said, (ch. 1: 2.) to have been carried
to Babylon, at the same time that Jeremiah informs
us, he was taken into Egypt, (Jer. 43: 6, 7.)

(3.) In 1 Maccabees, (8: 16,) it is asserted, that
"the Romans committed their government to one
man every year, who ruled over all that country, and
that all were obedient to that one; and that there was
neither envy nor emulation among them." This
assertion is contradicted by every Roman historian
that writes of those times.

(4.) The two Books of Maccabees directly contradict each other. For in one, (1 Macc. 6: 4–6,) Anti-
ochus Epiphanes is said to have died at Baby'on;
and in the other, (2 Macc. 1: 13–16,) he is represented
first, as having been slain by the priests in the Temple
of Nanea, in Persia; and afterwards as dying a miser-
able death in a strange country among the mountains.
(9: 28.)

Finally. The Apocrypha is rejected as uninspired,
because it contains many things that are evidently
false, fabulous, absurd, and contradictory to the
teachings of the Word of God.

The story of Bel and the Dragon, is confessedly, a
fiction. Judith is represented as justifying the slay-
ing of the Shechemites, which is, in the Bible,
explicitly condemed, (Gen. 49: 7.) The author of the
Book of Tobit, has added to the Scripture doctrines
concerning God and Providence, heathen superstitions
respecting dæmons or angels, intermediate between

God and man. And the angel that is introduced, is represented as telling a deliberate falsehood, (Tobit. 5: 12; 12: 15.) The expulsion of a dæmon by fumigation, (Tobit. 6: 1.) The conversion of fire into water, and *vice versa*, of water into fire, (2 Macc. 1: 19-22.) And the Tabernacle and the Ark walking after Jeremiah, at the Prophet's command, (2 Macc. 2; 4,) are stories utterly ridiculous and incredible. And finally, suicide, which is prohibited in the Bible, (Exod. 20; 13,) is in 2 Macc. 14: 41, mentioned with approbation.

For these and other sufficient reasons, the Apocrypha was rejected by Jerome, the learned translator of the Vulgate Latin, by St. Athanasius, and by the Council of Laodicea, (fourth Century,) which published a catalogue of the Inspired Books which were appointed to be read in public Worship. (*Horne's Introduction to the study of the Holy Scriptures.*)

It is difficult to imagine how writings thus marked by a character that seems almost calculated to bring Revelation itself, into contempt, should ever have been allowed to desecrate the volume containing the Word of God, unless it was permitted in the course of Divine Providence, to distinguish, with other infallible marks, the great Apostacy of Rome from the Church of the Living God.

16. *What use have some branches of the Christian Church, occasionally made of the Apocrypha?*—While the Church of Christ has uniformly and unanimously rejected the Apocrypha as forming no part of God's Inspired Word, yet some branches of the Church, since the fourth century, have thought it allowable to use some of these books "for example of life and instruction of manners;" but they have never been applied to establish the divine authority of any doctrine except by the Church of Rome.

The Standard Edition.

17. *Which is the third error of the Church of Rome respecting the Holy Scriptures?*—That which relates to the Edition of the Scriptures, to which, as the authoritative standard, all appeals in Theology are to be made; and all ecclesiastical questions determined.

18. *Which Edition of the Scriptures is thus adopted by the Church of Rome?*—"The Old Latin Vulgate Translation, which has been approved by its use in the (Papal) Church, for so many ages;" and "which no one shall dare or presume to reject, under any pretence whatever." (*Con. Trid. Dec. de Ed.*

19. *What may be observed of this remarkable preference of an uninspired and erroneous translation, to the inspired Scriptures in the original tongues?*—That it is one of the many instances in which the Papal Society has been permitted in their blindness, to bear testimony of their own free will, to their great diversity from the Church of the Living God.

20. *What is the doctrine of the general Christian Church upon this point?*—Although the Church of Christ holds, that to diffuse the knowledge of God, and to encourage the universal study of his Written Word, it is needful and right to translate the Scriptures into the vernacular tongue of all people to whom those Scriptures may be sent; yet in all controversies and questions in religion, the final appeal, is not to any translation, how accurate soever, it may be; but only to the Inspired Originals in the Hebrew and Greek Languages.

Infallible Interpretation.

21. *Which is the fourth error of the Church of Rome, respecting the Bible?*—That which arrogates to herself

the exclusive right to expound the Scriptures; and which maintains, that no one else has the right to search the Scriptures for himself or to understand them in a sense different from her teaching.

22. *How does the Church of Rome attempt to justify this monstrous claim of lordship over the Word of God, and over the minds and consciences of men?*—By the pretence, that their Popes and other Bishops are always guided in expounding the Word of God, by the same divine Spirit of infallibility, that was granted by our Lord to his holy Apostles; and that no other persons since the days of the Apostles, are so guided into all truth of religion. (*Milner's Catechism.*)

23. *How may we easily show the falsehood of this pretention to Infallibility?*—By the historic fact, that many Popes, Bishops, and Councils, have repeatedly contradicted and reversed the authoritative decrees of each other: while the whole Papal Society has, in so many particulars, violated the law and order of Christ's Church, as established by the Apostles, and as recorded in the Holy Scriptures, that it has well nigh forfeited all just claim to be considered a branch of the Christian Church. Certainly, *they who contradict each other, do not all speak the truth;* and that church or society, which statedly violates the express condition of Christ's promised presence, (Matt. 28: 18–20,) must boast in vain, the guidance of Christ's Spirit.

24. *What instances may be mentioned in illustration of this?*—(1.) Gregory the Great, who became Pope in the year A. D., 590, in reproving the ambition of his rival, the aspiring Patriarch of Constantinople, said: "He who calls himself *Universal Bishop*, or desires to be so called, is the forerunner of Anti-Christ!" But from the time of Pope Boniface III., the successor of Gregory, the Popes of Rome have

claimed universal supremacy in the Church, as the successors of Peter, and vicars of Christ.

(2.) In the year A. D. 1308, the seat of the popedom was removed from Rome to Avignon, which remained the pretended capital of The States of the Church, until A. D. 1378, when two Popes were elected, one at Avignon and the other at Rome. During the following period of schism and of fierce contenion, which continued for about fifty years, the Church had two, and sometimes, three Popes, each claiming to be the sole, supreme, infallible, successor of Peter; and each denouncing his rivals as impostors.

From the year A. D. 251, there are enumerated forty Anti-Popes; that is Popes, who on some ground of right, claimed the infallible popedom, in opposition to a similar claim on the part of their more successful competitors.

(3.) In the year A. D. 1590, Pope Sixtus V. published an edition of the Latin Vulgate Bible, and by an authoritative decree, commanded that it should be universally received as the "True, legitimate, authentic, undoubted, edition of the Holy Scriptures; and that all future editions should be conformed to it, without changing, adding, or omitting the least syllable, on pain of the greater excommunication." In utter contempt of the infallible Sixtus, and in disregard of his infallible decree, an infallible successor, Clement VIII. suppressed the infallible work of Sixtus, and published another infallible standard of the Scriptures, making in it more than two thousand corrections. (*Keary's Historical Review of Papal Infallibility.*)

(4.) Beside a general diversity from the Apostolic model of Christ's Church, the society which acknowledges the supreme headship of the Pope, is evidently not, as such, the kingdom of Christ, from the fact, that for many ages, and until recently, it was actually, and still claims to be, a temporal sovereignty, sustained like other kingdoms of this world, by force of arms. (John 18 : 36.)

25. *What is the doctrine of the Catholic Church of Christ, respecting the interpretation of the Holy Scriptures?*—(1.) That the infallible rule of Scripture interpretation, is the Scripture itself; when therefore, there is a question as to the true and full sense of any Scripture, it may be searched and known by other places that speak more clearly. (John 5: 39, 46; Acts 15 : 13–15.)

(2.) That the supreme judge by whom all controversies of religion are to be determined; and all decrees of councils, opinions of ancient writers, doctrines of men, and of private spirits, are to be examined, and in whose sentence we are to rest, can be no other than the Holy Spirit speaking in the Scripture. (Matt. 22 : 29–32; Acts 28; 25–29; Ephes 2 : 20.)

THE BIBLE RESTRICTED TO THE CLERGY.

26. *What is the fifth error of the Papal Church, respecting the Bible?*—That none but the clergy are required to read and study the Word of God; it being sufficient for the laity, that they listen to it from their pastors.

The laity, however, may be permitted to read the Scriptures, "but with due submission to the interpretation and authority of the Church."(*Milner's Catechism.*

27. *What are the doctrine and practice of the Church of Christ, on this point?*—That it is the privilege and duty of all classes of persons to search the Scriptures for their own edification, according to the direction of the blessed Redeemer, the great Prophet of the

Church, "Search the Scriptures." (John 5 : 39.)

28. *What may fairly be inferred from these Words of our Saviour?*—(1) That the Scriptures then extant, (The Old Testament,) were either in the possession of the persons addressed, or were easily accessible to them.

(2.) That the sense of those Scriptures was sufficiently perspicuous to the common intellect of men ; who are no where in the Word of God, subjected to the pretended infallibility of uninspired men.

(3.) That as the persons here addressed, were evidently an assemblage of mixed character, diverse attainments, and of various classes, the duty enjoined is not confined to any special class, as the clergy or the learned ; but is, without exception, the precious privilege of all sorts and conditions of men.

29. *How does it appear that the New Testament Scriptures, no less than those of the Old Testament, are to be possessed and studied by the common people?*—Not only on account of the superior light and liberty which distinguish the Gospel Dispensation ; but because the Christian Scriptures expressly declare themselves designed for the people generally, (*Design of the Bible*, p. 21.) And thus, while it is conceded, that it is the duty of the clergy to instruct the people out of the Holy Scriptures ; it is at the same time the corresponding duty of the people to examine for themselves, from the same Scriptures, what they hear from their pastors, (Acts. 17 : 11.)

THE BIBLE A DANGEROUS BOOK.

30. *What is the sixth and most remarkable error of the Church of Rome with respect to the Bible?*—That "numberless heresies and impieties ; as also many rebellions and civil wars," have "ensued from an unrestricted reading of the Bible, in vulgar languages,

by the *unlearned and unstable.*" (*Milner's Catechism.*)

31. *What may be replied to this extraordinary asser-tion?*—It is undoubtedly true, that from the time men have been enabled, by the unrestricted study of the Bible, in their respective languages, to understand their personal rights and duties, and their responsi-bility for their religion, to God alone; they have been generally, unwilling to submit to priestly dictation in matters of faith; and have, in many instances, taken up arms in defence of their Bible rights and privileges. But the guilt of all such "rebellions and civil wars," rests wholly with those ecclesiastical or civil rulers, whose audacity and tyranny rendered such "impie-ties" unavoidable. "It must needs be, that offences come, but wo to that man by whom the offence cometh." "When the strong man armed, (Romanism,) keepeth his court, his goods, (the poor people,) are in peace; but when a stronger than he, (the Bible,) cometh, it taketh away all his armor wherein he trusted." The Bible is indeed, a troublesome and dangerous Book to every system of error, oppression, and iniquity; but it is "The power of God unto salvation to every one that believeth."

32. *What opinions have been expressed by certain Romanists respecting the Bible, and its translation for the use of the common people?*—(1.) Henry Knyghton, a priest, writing of Wyclif's translation of the Bible, said: "This master John Wyclif has translated out of the Latin into English, the Gospel which Christ had entrusted with the clergy and doctors of the Church, that they might minister it to the laity and weaker sort, according to the exigency of times and their several occasions. So that by this means, the Gospel is made vulgar, and laid more open to the laity, and even to women that can read, than it used to be to the clergy, and those of the best understand-

ing. And so the Gospel Jewel, or evangelical pearl,
is thrown about and trodden under foot of swine."

(2.) Albert, archbishop and elector of Mentz, (A. D.
1530,) accidentally meeting with a Bible, opened it;
and having read some pages, observed: "Indeed I do
not know what this book is; but this I see *that every
thing in it is against us.*"

(3.) A council of Romish bishops assembled at Bon-
onia, October, 1553, for the purpose of advising Pope
Julius III. as to the best means of checking the progress
of the Reformation; said among other things: "This
book, (the Bible,) is that which has beyond all other
books, raised these storms and tempests in which we
are almost driven to destruction. And really, whosoever shall diligently weigh the Scripture, and then
consider all the things that are usually done in our
churches, will find that there is a great difference
between them; and that this doctrine of ours is very
unlike, and in many things, quite repugnant to it."

"Oppositions of Science, Falsely so-called."

1. *What theories have been advanced in opposition to
the Bible account of the Creation of all things, of Nothing?*
Certain ancient philosophers denied the doctrine of
"creation from nothing;" their favorite maxim being:
"Ex nihilo nihil fit,"—"Nothing can be produced from
nothing." Some of them maintained the existence of
two eternal principles: An active spirit, (God,) and
passive matter. That this eternal spirit operating
upon eternal matter, formed the present visible universe; and that the souls of men, as well as angels,
and other spiritual beings, were not created, but
are emanations from the eternal spirit.

(2.) Others, with some among the moderns, denying that the universe was created, held, that the
present existence and order of things are the acciden-

tal result of certain vital forces. or laws of nature, operating by chance, upon a heterogeneous mass of atoms which have always existed.

(3.) Another scheme, of more recent date, attempts to account for the present order of things, by supposing that all forms of vegetable, and animal life have proceeded, by a constant "evolution," from an original "germ," under the controling influence of a principle, named "natural selection."

2. *What may be observed of all such theories?*—(1.) That they are mere speculations, unsustained by evidence sufficient to secure their general reception by the learned.

(2.) They do not account for the order, symmetry, and the correlations which prevail throughout the universe ; nor do they satisfactorily explain the origin of anything. (3.) None of the more recent of these schemes of cosmogony are original inventions; but are in fact, modifications of the old mythologies of Orpheus, Zoroaster, or of Epicurus. (*Enfield's Hist. of Phil.*)

3. *How do the Scriptures account for the origin of the universe, and of the various orders and classes of beings which compose it?*—(1.) That all things "were framed by the word of God, so that things which are seen, were not made of things which do appear." (Heb. 11: 3.) (2.) that God at the first, gave to each order and class of things, a distinct and specific nature, each "after its kind." (Gen. 1: 21 ; 2: 5, 7.)

(3.) And the design of the vast and beautiful fabric of the universe is set forth by the Apostle. in the following impressive language: "For by Him, (God's dear Son, Jesus Christ,) were all things created, that are in heaven, and that are in earth, visible and invisible, whether they be thrones, or dominions, or principalities, or powers; all things were created by

Him and for Him." (Col. 1 : 16 ; Heb. 1 : 1—3.)

4. *What theories of the earth have been urged against the Scripture account of the creation of all things in the space of six days ?*—Those of the modern Geologis's, in which they maintain, that the present condition of the crust of the earth, (extending to the depth of about twenty or thirty miles,) is the result of agencies that have been in operation for unknown thousands of years. That therefore, the world is much older than appears from the record of Moses, literally understood. And that the six days of creation are not literally six natural days, but designate, figuratively, six great successive periods, each of many thousands of years.

5. *What may be replied to this?*—*First*, as Moses does not attribute the work of creation to an incompetent power, but narrates in the language of simple continuous history, the production of all things, by the hand of omnipotence, there is nothing incredible or improbable in the statement.

Secondly. As the literal sense of the language of the inspired writer, is the most obvious and natural, it must be so received, unless there were some reason stated or alluded to, why it should be otherwise understood. But there is not the least hint suggested in any part of the Bible, that would lead us to suspect that the statements of Moses respecting the creation, are to be understood in a metaphorical, symbolical, or mythological sense.

On the contrary, there is expressly stated, as the reason of the Fourth Commandment, (Ex. 20 : 11,) a positive fact, which, taken in connection with the "evening and the morning" of Genesis. (Ch. 1 : 5.) imperatively determines the six days of creation, to have been six natural days of twenty-four hours each.

Thirdly. While we know perfectly, the philological

principles needful to explain the language of the inspired narrative of the creation, considered as simple history ; we do not know certainly, the nature of the principles required to explain all the admitted facts of Geology.

Fourthly. While we admit all the facts of Geology, we must be careful to distinguish between those facts and the theories that have been advanced to explain them. The facts as they exist in the earth, do not necessarily explain themselves, as to the process and date of their accompiishment. For examp'e, it is affirmed, that certain rocks were formed by chemical affinity, modified by the action of fire, water, pressure, volcanic force, &c. Now admitting this, it still remains possible, that other rocks, were created just as we find them. Appearances, however, are not always reliable, as the basis of an argument. If the dead body of the first man had been dissected, doubtless, there would have been found the same organs, the same appearance and arrangement of bones, muscles, arteries, &c., identically as they are found, to-day, in any subject of the dissecting room. In like manner, the examination of a primitive oak, immediately after its creation, would have presented the identical appearance of bark, woody fibre, leaves, acorns, &c., just as we find the oak in our forests to-day. So of the rocks. *If therefore, the appearances of chemical action* in the rocks, determine that they were not created as we find them; then, *the appearances of growth to maturity,* in the first man, and in the first oak tree, lead with equal force to the conclusion, that they were not created as asserted by Moses.

To account, therefore, for the facts of any physical science, we are not justified in adopting a theory at variance with the clear and long admitted sense of an authentic record.

Fifthly. There is no principle of any physical science, ascertained and admitted by the learned, *which renders impossible*, the production of all the facts of Geology, within the historic period of six thousand years, beginning with the six natural days of the creation.

Finally. We are not certain that we have discovered all the facts of Geology. The bosom of the earth may still embrace other facts, far more interesting and astonishing than any thing hitherto discovered; and which, when compared with what we already know, may furnish an explanation of the whole subject in accordance with the historic narrative of Moses, as heretofore, commonly understood. It is the part, therefore, of sound philosophy, as well as that of humble piety, to seek for more light upon the facts of Geology, while with respect to the Word of God, we continue in the old paths of safe and simple truth.

5. *What is the relation of the Bible to the Science of Astronomy?*—The sacred writers that allude to that interesting subject, show, that like all other thoughtful men of every age from the beginning, they fully appreciated the glory and grandeur of the starry firmament, (Psal. 19 : 1–6,) and the comparative insignificence of man and the world he occupies, (Psal. 8 : 3, 4.) And that while they evidently understood the great principles of Astronomy which were known in their day, (Job. 9 : 9; 26 : 7; 38 : 31,) and which have been confirmed and elaborated by later discoveries; they speak of the "rising" and "going down" of the sun, and of other celestial phenomena, (Eccles. 1 : 6; Psal. 119 : 90,) in the familiar language of popular observation. In this, they have been followed by professional astronomers and by all mankind, in speaking of the same phenomena, in every age to the present. If therefore, the sacred writers in this,

are guilty of contradicting science; then Kepler and
Galileo, Newton, Herschell, and Brewster, fall under
the same condemnation.

All that is affirmed by the sacred writers, relative
to the creation of the countless, starry host, by the
word of God, challenges contradiction. The discoveries in modern Astronomy are wonderful beyond
conception; but nothing yet brought to light, is inconsistent with the pious declaration: "Of old hast
thou laid the foundation of the earth, and the heavens
are work of thy hands." (Psal. 102 : 25.)

The inspired writers, however, do not confine their
testimony to the *creation and preservation* of the
heavens and the earth, by the infinite Being, whose
servants they were; but they declare also, in his
sovereign name, *the future destruction* of all these
vast and beautiful things, by the hand that made
them; in order to bring forth a "new heavens and a
new earth!" (2 Pet. 3 : 10–13; Heb. 1 : 10, 11.)   Now
while the superficial star-gazer may imagine he sees
evidences in the bright orbs above, inconsistent with
the doctrine of a divine creation; no well informed
astronomer, will for an instant hesitate in admitting
the possibility of the predicted destruction of the
earth by fire; for his trusted telescope has revealed
the same or similar phenomena in other worlds. (*Dun-
kin's Midnight Sky, p.* 154.)

6. *What then, is the proper conclusion of the long
agitated questions between the Bible and physical science?*
(1.) That between the Word of God and the Works
of God, there can be no actual contradiction; any
apparent discrepancy between them, must therefore,
be due to our ignorance of the one or of the other.

(2.) Assuming, then, the essential harmony between
Nature and Revelation; let the believer, accept, without hesitation, all the discoveries of true science as the

best confirmation of his faith. And let the votary of science, as he pierces the earth to learn the lesson of the rocks, fail not to build his eternal hope upon "The Rock of Ages."—"The chief Corner Stone laid in Zion." And as he explores the firmament, to resolve the profound mysteries of the stellar universe, let him first of all, "determine the elements" of that "bright, particular star," which has neither "right ascension," "parallax," nor "declination."—"Jesus Christ, the same yesterday, to-day, and forever."

May the ever blessed God, by his Holy Spirit, give us grace so to read the Book of Nature, that we may the more highly prize the Book of Inspiration; the one, the revelation of infinite Power; the other, of inffnite Love! Reading both volumes aright, we shall, by the grace of God, find no difficulty in understanding, why "God so loved the world, that he gave his only begotten Son, that whosoever believeth in him should not perish, but have everlasting life;" and, no reason, either to be alarmed at the progress of true science, or to be "ashamed of the gospel of Christ."

APPENDIX.

Note *A.*—Sir Isaac Newton.

Sir Isaac Newton was fully persuaded of the existence of God, understanding by that term, not only an infinite, almighty, eternal, creative, power; but also, a personal Being—a Master—who has established a relation between himself and his creatures: as without this relation, the knowledge of a God is only a barren idea, which would seem to invite every reasoner of a perverse nature to the practice of vice, by the hope of impunity. Accordingly, that great philosopher makes this singular remark: "We do not say, 'my eternal,' my infinite'; because those attributes do not relate to our nature. But we say: 'My God,' understanding thereby the author and preserver of our life, the object of our thought and adoration."

Newton's philosophy leads directly to the knowledge of a supreme Being, who freely created and arranged all things. "If," says he, "the planets, in space void of resistence, revolve one way, rather than another, the hand of their Creator must have directed them that way with absolute freedom."

Note *B.*—Inspiration.

The gift of inspiration, or that divine in-breathing, under which the Scriptures were written, was distinct from the work of the Spirit in regeneration; although it was enjoyed, for the most part, only by such as were effectually called by divine grace. And it was distinct also, from those miraculous gifts of the Spirit granted to converts in the Apostolic age, by which they wrought miracles, and spake with tongues, (Acts, 10: 46; 19: 6; 1 Cor. 12: 8–11.) Those gifts were indeed, enjoyed by them who were 'inspired to write'; but they were possessed and exercised, a'so, by multitudes who were not so inspired. Those general gifts of the Spirit were evidently designed for the benefit of that primitive period, that the truth of the Gospel might be impressively and rapidly diffused; and with the occasion, the gifts themselves ceased. But the special inspiration of the sacred penmen, was that peculiar influence of the Holy Spirit, by which they were qualified and directed to commit wholly unto writing, the whole counsel of God for the salvation and comfort of his Church, and for a testimony against his embittered foes in all ages to the end.

Note *C*.—MIRACLES.

In the following passages of Scripture, among others, all power to perform miracles is appropriated exclusively to Jehovah, the only living and true God: Exod. 7: 17; 9: 14; 15: 11; Deut. 4: 32–36; Ps. 136: 4. And the uniform testimony of Scripture, is that God alone has the inherent power to raise the dead, (Deut. 32: 39; John 5: 25–29; 2 Cor. 1: 9.) To open the eyes of the blind, (Ps. 146: 8; John 9: 1–7.) To tread on the waves of the sea, (Job 9: 8; Mark 6: 48–51.) To still the noise of its waves, Ps. 65: 9; Matt. 8: 23–27.) To reveal secret things, (Dan. 2: 28, 29, 47: John 4: 16–19.) To foretell the future, (Isa. 42: 9; Matt. ch. 24.) And to search the heart of man, (Jer. 17: 9, Luke 5: 22.) And thus the Scriptures, in claiming for Jehovah, exclusive possession of miraculous power, as the peculiar prerogative of the Godhead, deny in the most emphatic manner, that any such power is poss ssed by angelic beings, either good or bad, by the spirits of departed men, by heathen deities, by magicians who pretended to hold intercourse with them; and finally, by all false prophets, upon what princ:ple soever, they may found their pretensions. A miracle, then, is a special act wrought at the wi l, command, or prayer of the prophet, in testimony of his divine mission; but it is accomplished only by "the finger of God."

Note *D.*—PROPHECY.

The fulfilment of a prophecy, is in the Scriptures, (Deut. 18: 21; 1 Samuel 3: 19, 20; Isa. 41: 24; Jer. 28: 9; Ezek. 23: 33,) expressly declared to be the direct and specific evidence, that "The Lord hath spoken it." And since the Scriptures profess to be the record of both prophecy and its fulfilment, we may perceive the vital importance of the question of their credibility. To the candid mind, this question is, in effect, determined by the argument drawn from the coincidence between the prophecies and the history of the Bible. Indeed, the historical portions of the Bible, are to a great extent, narratives of events previously foretold. The New Testament particularly, is essentially the record of the accomplishment of the predictions and types of the Old Testament, respecting the Lord Jesus Christ, his great salvation, and his blood-bought Church. So intimate is the connection of the two Testaments, in this respect, that they mutually prove the truth and inspiration of each other, and jointly demonstrate, in opposition to all infidelity, that they bear the image and superscription of Jehovah.

Note *E.*—The Testimony of the Life of Christ.

In the most approved systems of philosophy ever devised by man for the promotion of either individual or social happiness, in all the laws for the maintenance of virtue, either private or public, there has been wanting on the part of the philosopher or law-giver, a practical illustration of the wisdom and virtue he would recommend to others. Mere human teaching has ever failed to illustrate perfectly its own precepts in living example. In this respect the Gospel of Christ claims to be peculiar; and so peculiar as to demand universal assent to its claim of divine origin. In the personal life and character of Jesus of Nazareth, as recorded by the Evangelists, there is portrayed a perfect model of human virtue and greatness, according to the exalted standard of his own pure morality. In every act of his life his character is fully sustained; in every sentiment expressed, his enemies seek in vain to entrap him; his wisdom and purity are upon all occasions, conspicious; and at the bar of judicial investigation, "his enemies themselves being judges," he is acquitted of all fault!

In the Blessed Jesus we behold the docility and meekness of the child, the affection and fidelity of the sympathizing friend and brother; parental tenderness to the young, condescension and grace to the poor, reassuring mercy to the erring and penitent; and to his determined foes, a fearlessness, forbearance, patience, dignity, and self-possession, beyond the exercise of mere humanity. Though he knew the law perfectly, "he knew no sin;" his whole life, from the beginning to the end of it, was "holy, harmless, and separate from sinners;" and "no guile was found in his mouth."

A character so well sustained throughout, so entirely free from all imperfection; and withal, so completely illustrative of his own precepts and principles, is certainly a remarkable phenomenon in human biography. It is, indeed, the only instance of the kind on record. The great reformers, phi'osophers, and heroes of other histories, were far different men from Jesus of Nazareth; while the divinities of mythology were, for the most part, monsters of humanity, the exaggerations of lawless and abandoned men. That it were possible for the Evangelists to conceive such a character as that of our Redeemer, they must have had a living model. To record it as they have done, they must have been divinely inspired; and had they not in their narrative asserted the proper divinity of their hero, as well as his true humanity, their testimony would have been wholly incredible; for had the Son of Mary been a mere man, the Christ of the Gospel would have been an impossibility.

Note F.—Magic Arts.

The wonders wrought by the magicians of Egypt were mere imitations of the miracles of Moses, accomplished by human artifice and slight-of-hand jugglery. This is all that can be fairly inferred from the texts, (Exod. 7: 11; 8: 18, &c.,) which state indeed, that after a miracle had been wrought by Moses, the magicians "did so with their enchantments." But this cannot mean any thing more than that they succeeded in producing some kind of an imitation of what Moses and Aaron had done; for in relation to the plague of lice, it is said in the same language, "They did so with their enchantments, to bring forth lice, but they could not." That they did not, in any of their efforts in withstanding Moses, pretend to be assisted by any god, or being superior to themselves, is evident from what they declared of this plague:

"This is the finger of God;" or, "of a god." And it is evident that the Witch of Endor, although professing to be able to raise the dead and converse with them, did not really expect to raise up Samuel or any one else, from her alarm and consternation at the sight of Samuel, who appeared before she had time to practice any of the usual rites and ceremonies of the wicked art which she professed. And it is equally evident, that the prophet Samuel was miracuously raised by God's special power, both to confound the Witch in her art of imposture; and to denounce the divine judgment against Saul, not only for his previous sins; but especially for this last aggravated offence against God's Law, in coming to consult a familiar spirit, (Deut. 18 : 9–12 ; 1 Samuel, chapter 28 ; 1 Chron. 10: 13.) The distinction between Miracles and Magic is further illustrated in the case of Simon Magus, (Acts 8 : 5–13.

Note *G.*—A Mahometan.

Mr. J. S. Buckingham, relates the following:
"Happening to be travelling with a caravan from Morocco to Mecca, on the way down, I was a good deal in the society of an intelligent mahometan merchant, a native of Fez, in Morocco. His being on a pilgrimage to the "Holy City," was a sufficient proof that he was a zealous and staunch believer in the mamometan religion. Having ascertained that he would listen, without being offended to any objections I might make to his religion, I asked him if it had ever occurred to him, that his religion was not intended to be universal, and that it could not possibly be universally adopted. He replied that this idea had never occurred to him; and that could this be proved, it would shake his confidence in the divine origin of his religion ; for it would not be reasonable to require

all mankind to do that which could be done by only a part of the human family."

"Well," I replied, "you mahometans are as ignorant of geography as you are of most other things, otherwise you would know that there are countries where there is sun-light six months in the year, and darkness the other six; in other words, the sun is six months above the horizon without setting; and then six months below the horizon, without rising; so that there is but one day and one night in the whole year. Now every mahometan is expressly enjoined, during the Ramadan, to abstain from every article of meat and drink, from the rising to the setting of the sun; an injunction plainly impossible, in the countries I have named. He said, it was impossible there could be such parts of the world. But I demonstrated the fact to him, and the argument so affected him, that instead of continuing his pilgrimage to the templ,e at Mecca, the object of his long and weary journey, he stopped at Jedda; and having transacted some business, abandoned his pilgrimage, and returned to Fez.

THE REVISED VERSION.

The revision of the English Authorized Translation of the Bible, of 1611, originated in the Convocation of Canterbury, February, 1870. The work of revising the New Testament was commenced on the 22d day of June, 1870, by the Committee appointed by the Convocation of Canterbury; and with the co-operation of a committee of American scholars, it was completed, November, 11th, 1880. In May, 1881, it was published to the world; and the universal demand for copies, gave abundant evidence, if any were needed, that THE BIBLE IS THE BOOK OF THE PEOPLE.

INDEX.

www.ingramcontent.com/pod-product-compliance
Lightning Source LLC
Chambersburg PA
CBHW022152090426
42742CB00010B/1484